I0539147

FINDING
The Word
MADE FLESH

FINDING
The Word
MADE FLESH

DENNIS L. COPENHAVER

ARPress
ILLUMINATING IDEAS,
EMPOWERING VOICES

Copyright © 2025 by Dennis L. Copenhaver.

All rights reserved. No part of this publication may be reproduced, distributed, or transmitted in any form or by any means, including photocopying, recording, or other electronic or mechanical methods, without the prior written permission of the copyright owner and the publisher, except in the case of brief quotations embodied in critical reviews and certain other noncommercial uses permitted by copyright law. For permission requests, write to the publisher, addressed "Attention: Permissions Coordinator," at the address below.

ARPress
45 Dan Road Suite 5
Canton MA 02021

Hotline: 1(888) 821-0229
Fax: 1(508) 545-7580

Ordering Information:
Quantity sales. Special discounts are available on quantity purchases by corporations, associations, and others. For details, contact the publisher at the address above.

Printed in the United States of America.

ISBN-13:   Softcover   979-8-89676-326-0
            eBook   979-8-89676-327-7

Library of Congress Control Number: 2025902992

Table of Contents

Acknowledgements...vii

Introduction...ix

Dreams Of Flying 1

Seeking Christ Among Christians 3

Growing Up 11

Real Christians 13

The Day That Changed My Life..15

Doubts...19

Feed My Sheep...21

ACKNOWLEDGEMENTS

This is the first book I have typed myself on a computer and I wish to thank Adele Smith for encouraging me to do it this way. I also want to thank my daughter, Jennifer, for her help setting up the computer as I struggle to learn something new to me. But most of all I want to thank all the Christians over the years who answered questions for me and discussed faith with me at length. Without them I would not have this story to tell. Last of all I thank the Lord for coming to Earth to give us the hope of eternal life through the Son, Jesus.

INTRODUCTION

This is my story of my search for the real Jesus. It has a rather slow beginning as a child then adolescent who struggled to learn right from wrong. After all, who defines right and wrong? Or truth? Does it really depend on who you ask or how old they are? As a child, I knew my father's mother, Florence. She flatly stated repeatedly that she loves the Lord and had read the bible "cover to cover" three times while she was in a tuberculosis asylum for seven years.

Florence had only gone to the sixth grade in school and used a backward country version of English, so my first thought was "You didn't understand it the first or second time, so you read it again?" but I never said that out loud out of 'respect for my elders.' By age six, I knew that lack of respect would get me corrected and if not lucky, a slap across the mouth by my other elders, but not Grandma Florence. This kind, forgiving woman was my first example of a Christian Lady but at the time, I just thought of her as a senile old woman. My attitude was totally wrong, and I regret my own thoughts to this day.

She was a gift from God, there to show me an example and I did not get it at the time. I think of her now as smiling down on me from heaven and happy to see me reading my bible (I've only read it once, 'cover to cover'). My search for my own faith was long and sometimes complicated, but hopefully worth telling.

DREAMS OF FLYING

In my Grandmother Florence's house was a very old and large print on the wall of a little boy and a little girl hand-in -hand crossing a rickety old footbridge on a dark and storm day. Above them, hovering in midair, was an adult figure with beautiful large wings holding its hands over them.

When I asked Grandma why the adult had wings and could fly, she said, "That's the children's Guardian Angel!" So, I was introduced to the winged messengers who could fly, as well as sing their messages to people.

After hearing of angels and seeing artwork like that, I started having recurring dreams of flying. In my dreams, the wind on the ridge tops would blow strong and steady and I would spread my wings and lift off the ground and soar like an eagle! I flew all over my hometown neighborhood and farms. What a beautiful view I had both daytime and sometimes at sunset.

I would be a young adult before I actually got to fly and see the ground from above only to see it looked exactly like my childhood dreams --- the view of rooftops and chimneys, the people so small below they looked like ants and cars like small toys!

My favorite thing about the dreams of flying was feeling the air rush past my face and wings. In my dreams, I would extend my arms and the wings would extend. Descent was done by changing the angle of my arms, steering by moving one arm at a time.

I never told anyone of my dreams of flying. I remember thinking: "Am I a bird or a type of angel? What am I? Humans don't fly, but every dream made me yearn for another dream with a steady wind so I could soar again!

The flying dreams became recurrent, maybe greater than twenty times. I used to wake up and wonder why I dream of flying. I always felt like I had really flown before --- before what? Now I am older and realize that I saw wings on Grandma's angel and wished I could fly.

As a child, I used to search for hours, like something was missing or lost. I would grow tired and sad for I could not find what I was searching for. Sometimes I cried tears of frustration. What was I looking for? Something from the past? Something that does not exist?

As I got older, the dreams stopped. Reality took over. I learned to accept only what could be proven. After all, I had never seen a real angel, just artwork. Later I saw many depictions of angels. I even saw an entire book filled with artist's renditions of, "The Face of Jesus", but no photos of either – there are none.

Then Florence's comments came back to me: "Every man and woman sees Jesus in their own mind. He has been seen with many different colors of skin, eyes, hair, and styles of hair. Many see Jesus as one of their nation. Same way with angels. That's why every painting is different." Wow! Not bad for a person with a sixth-grade education!

My dreams of flying were gone forever. Reality checking became a wall. I had built the wall but did not know it would become a wall between me and faith. I believed in what I could see and touch and prove. Nothing in my world ever came back from the dead. Not plants, not animals, and certainly not humans. My feet stayed on the ground, I never soared again. My faith wanted to grow but it could not soar also. My mind demanded proof. I remember wishing that Jesus were still here so I could follow him around like the disciples. I felt totally drawn to Jesus's teachings. I started to search for him in people who believe in him.

SEEKING CHRIST AMONG CHRISTIANS

Christians is the term we apply to people who believe in and follow the teachings of Christ. I used to think of all Christians as the same. I had no awareness that followers of Christ had all kinds of different levels of faith and understanding. As people, we pick and choose what we believe, especially in what others teach or state they believe. No wonder there are so many denominations today! I guess that I am a product of my times.

When I look back on my life, I can see a series of meeting people who helped me develop my faith and desire to be closer to Jesus starting about age ten. My parents became convinced that I needed help to better learn right from wrong at that age. Most of their concern stemmed from conflict with my only brother, Bill, who was one year younger than me. I remember being dressed in identical clothes a lot, so everyone thought we were twins. They even cut our hair the same length and style. People knew us as "Butch" and "Billy" but about half did not know us apart.

I became unhappy when I wanted people to see us as individuals, different from each other. I did not want to be beside him 24 hours a day! (We even slept in the same bed!). We did have some different likes and dislikes, but I was forced to play with him, never by myself. Personal space and alone time did not exist.

That lead to conflicts and fighting. I once choked Bill so bad that he was turning purple by the time Mom stopped me. At that time, I was so young that I did not know that I could have hurt him.

A few weeks later we were playing "Cowboys and Indians". We took turns being the cowboy or Indian. When it was my turn to be the Indian, I sneaked up behind Bill and pretended to stab him with a knife. It was actually a broken old-fashioned clothes pin with one prong missing that I held by the top as a handle. I never actually touched him with it and the end was round and not sharp at all. He played his part and gasped falling backward to the ground. Unfortunately, he struck the top corner of a cement platform and knocked himself out cold! The corner cut all the way to his skull and the deep scalp wound bled profusely!

I screamed for help and the older kids who were playing baseball in a nearby field came running followed by the adults. The adults grabbed Bill and jumped into a car to go to the nearest doctor. They left me with the older teenage kids.

Then it started! From where they were playing, they thought they saw me stab Bill. I showed them blood on the cement corner and none on my play knife, but they did not care. They insisted I would be taken to jail when the adults returned, found guilty of murder if Bill died, and probably be put to death! They could not decide if they would hang me or put me in an electric chair! They really laid it on thick and seemed to enjoy terrifying me.

When the adults came home, they spent hours looking for me as I had hidden myself in Grandma Bish's root cellar. They said they believed me but decided to get me taught right from wrong before I killed someone! I guess the local gossip was buzzing about me. People were believing the negative stories!

So that weekend on a beautiful spring Sunday morning, Mom drove me to a Methodist church about a half mile away and pointed to a door and said, "Go in there and ask for a lady named Bobby Traister!"

Bobby was a young lady and very nice. She took me to a small room, just her and me, and started by telling me all the bad that can happen to people that hurt others. When she got to the hellfire and brimstone when bad people die, I started to cry! She had to calm me down and said she wanted to talk to me about Jesus Christ.

I said, "Oh no! I'm not allowed to swear!! That's what Grandpa Bish says when he hits his thumb with the hammer! The first time I said that when I hit my thumb, Grandma Bish washed my mouth out with soap! I'm not allowed to swear!". I thought his name was just swear words.

It took a while, but I really came to like the Jesus that Bobby told me about. She was my first Sunday school teacher and laid the foundation that my faith built upon and I credit her for leading me to Jesus and helping to save my soul. What is really wonderful is that she is still alive, and I have told her what she did for me when I saw her several years ago. She is in her nineties now and I hope to give her a copy of this book if I get it published. Bobby was the first of many mentors and teachers that I mentioned in my introduction.

Soon afterward, I met Francis Boozer who believed strongly in the healing power of prayer. She would drop to her knees and pray for anyone, anytime. Her husband, Cliff had a severely injured eye one day and my dad pulled on her arms and said, "Get up Francis, I got to get Cliff to a doctor now!"

Francis said, "Bill STOP! I have to pray for Cliff!"

Dad shouted, "Just get in the truck and keep his eye covered and you can pray the whole way to the hospital!" Then they left, and Francis was praying, and Dad said she did pray the whole way, but Cliff's eye and vision were saved that day.

About one year later, I thanked Francis for her cookies (boy, could she bake!), and I begged her to please take her blood pressure pills as I did not want her to die of a stroke. She said she was praying about her blood pressure. My Dad told her that God put doctors on this earth to help believers like her! She still refused the pills. Sadly, Francis died one year later of a stroke. My praying cookie baker was gone, and I cried. I did not know that I would become a Physician Assistant and practice for 33 ½ years in the future. I always had a soft spot for people like Francis and folks would drive for miles to see the "Christian Doctor".

I grew up hearing stories of Grandma and Grandpa Bish (Jack and Martha), my Mom's parents. Jack did not go to any church, but he fell in love with Martha, a Catholic girl. They married outside the Church, and she and her priest had words about the marriage. She stopped going to church over that. She made sure her grandchildren said grace before meals and bedtime prayers but that was the extent of our home Christian teaching until I went to the Methodist Church.

I attended two "Masses" with my Catholic best friend in high school, Nick Bain. He was also my Best Man when I married Cynthia, herself a Catholic, in 1976. My Grandpa Bish would not answer any questions about religion and I quickly learned not to ask. However, one day when I was about twelve years old, he and I were on a country drive on a Sunday afternoon. He suddenly slammed on the brake, backed our car up, and pointed to a large park in the woods. There were dozens of parked cars and picnic tables full of people of all ages. There must have been well over one hundred people!

Grandpa surprised me! He said, "There Denny, look at that and don't ever forget it! Those people all belong to the Catholic Church here and they really take care of each other! Look how happy they are." After a few minutes, we drove on in silence. He said nothing else.

So, I grew up knowing my ancestors on Mom's side of the family were Catholics and that they, the Catholics, were a closely knit group based on their beliefs. That was all I knew of the Catholic Church. Later I learned that all the other Christian churches had split off from the Catholics after a priest named Martin Luther sought to reform the church.

As I grew up, I would have many examples of Christian faith by people of different denominations. Each denomination seemed to focus on some aspect of faith or view of what was a sin or what was not. I was amazed by the variety of beliefs but one central belief: Jesus! All Christians believe in Jesus. Early on, I thought they meant his teachings. Later I learned that the "Resurrection" means he is still alive, and that belief is central to being truly "Christian". It occurred to me that I had been going to church for years but was struggling to find the living Christ!

I felt like a church going herd follower of Jesus. Jesus: A person I could not see or touch. My need for proof started to nag at me. I had started a quest and I could not stop! I felt like a knight sent out to find the holy grail. How does one find the living Christ? I felt I was getting glimpses in the faithful people I knew, but I felt I really needed to experience the living Lord! I can identify with Saint Thomas a lot! He was the disciple who had to see Jesus after the resurrection before he could believe. He had to see and feel the wounds to believe he was alive again.

When I was home on leave from the military, I would visit another special couple, Helen Songer, and her husband Fred. Helen had been one of my English teachers in junior high school and she and her husband attended the Methodist church that my Mother and I attended at that time. Both were very supportive of me and I could visit and discuss any subject with them.

It took me a while before I asked Helen one day, "What makes you guys so different from everyone else I know?"

She answered, "I suppose it's because we are both Christians and believe in the risen Lord!"

I asked, "How do you know he is still alive?"

She responded, "I feel it in my heart and soul. I know he lives!"

I almost said out loud, "Wish I could feel that way!"

They were both close friends, and I kept in touch while I was a cadet at the USAF Academy in Colorado and later in the Air Force. I remember sending Helen a card: "To My Other Mother" on Mothers' Day. Their faith was a strong influence on me!

They contrasted with some of the challenges I had faced. Something happened between me and my father that made me choose a path to follow. My father had never attended church, but he had agreed with Mom to sending me to church to "be taught right from wrong!" Of course, as a kid at Sunday school and summer Vacation Bible school, I had learned the "Ten Commandments". We had to recite them from memory.

One evening, after having attended Sunday school for about two years, my Father woke me up and said, "Get dressed, I need you boys to help me." Turns out it was me, my brother Bill, and my cousin Bob, an older teenager. We three were to help Dad. We got into his pickup with some tools and he would not tell us where we were going in the middle of the night. He drove for over an hour then backed his pickup to a chain link fence. I saw a locked gate and a security light but nobody there except us. Dad quickly cut a hole in the fence with bolt cutters, backed the truck through and said, "Now load her up, whatever I tell you to load. Work quick and quiet, no talking!"

With four people working, it did not take long. We loaded wood, buckets of nails, paint, roofing, etc. All building supplies! We were finishing up by shoveling on as much gravel as the truck could now hold when I suddenly stopped working.

"Dad! What are we doing? Who owns all this stuff?"

"The State does." He flatly said.

"So, we are doing this at night without a key because we do not have permission to take this stuff, do we?"

"It's OK son!" he said. "They steal our money through taxes, and we are just stealing some of it back!"

I dropped my shovel, "Dad, I can't do this!"

"Why the hell not?! Just do as I say!"

"Because Dad, 'Thou shall not steal.' is one of the Ten Commandments! I must follow all Ten Commandments, or I can't be a Christian!"

My Dad's face got cherry red! He was very upset. Usually, when his face gets red, someone gets hurt! He picked up my shovel. I actually thought he was going to hit me with the shovel. He was so big and strong and angry. He could have killed me in his anger, and I was too small to stop him. I had time to think "Lord, help me please!" and I closed my eyes.

Then I heard my father say, "Go sit in the truck and keep your mouth shut to the others. Now!"

So, I did what he said, and he finished shoveling and we went home to unload and go back to bed. They could all sleep in. It was Sunday tomorrow, and I would walk to church alone, as usual. I tried hard not to cry in church. I kept my mouth shut out of shame.

A day later, I overheard a conversation between my father and mother. "I want to tell Dennis he does not need to go to church anymore." Then he told Mom what had happened. "I want this to stop," he said. "He's in danger of getting religion!"

"Well Bill, what did you expect? We forced him to go to church remember?!" Mom growled. Then she left the room.

That afternoon, Dad informed me that I no longer had to go to Sunday school. I said, "OK, thanks. But what if I want to keep going?"

"That's your business, but we will not be taking you. When the weather is bad or winter comes, you'll change your mind."

Nine months later, I was still walking the ½ mile to church and back in all kinds of weather. Then, for some reason, Mom started to drive me in bad weather and even stayed a few times. I never asked her, she just got up and offered to go with me. Mom is 90 years old now and I still take her to the Methodist church on Sundays.

GROWING UP

When I was twelve years old, we moved back to my Dad's farm. My parents told me that we had lived there from my birth until I was three years old. From age three to twelve, we had lived next door to Grandma and Grandpa Bish at Widnoon, PA. Grandma spent many hours helping to raise us during this time. Grandma Bish had grown up Catholic but stopped going to church when she married Grandpa who did not attend or belong to any church. She and my mother taught us basic prayers before meals and at bedtime. The last couple years in Widnoon, Mother and I attended the United Methodist Church at Widnoon. Each little town in Pennsylvania had one or more little church of various denominations.

School was public and had students from every background: white collar, blue collar worker kids, and quite a few kids from poverty level too. Guess we were 'blue collar poor!' It was probably true that the majority of students did not attend any church on a regular basis. I remember that we had our share of aggressive kids and bullies! I had a particular problem as I had evolved a fear of hurting others. I had listened to teachings of: Turn the other cheek! Do not strike back! Instead be kind to others. What I got was beat up a lot! "Watch this! This guy will not hit back!", usually followed by a painful punch or slap. They saw anger in my eyes, but I would walk away if they let me. This happened when there was no adult around. I have no memory of anyone stopping the harassment. It continued until I suddenly "bloomed late", got size, muscle, and facial hair and the strength to hurt back. I also went into military training after high school and learned hand to hand combat and boxing. I boxed my second year at the USAF Academy and won nine out of ten matches. Nobody in their right mind wanted to fight me in the ring. My father bragged about my fighting ability, and no person has ever assumed that I would not defend myself ever since.

Being different can be a blessing and a curse at the same time. Following the Lord does not mean that others around you live by the same beliefs. Many people grow up with others who lie to them and lying becomes almost a habit. That is just one example. Stealing, cheating, etc. are all practiced in our society. Many may be attracted to you as a 'good person' when you follow Jesus. As we get older, we realize that these are opportunities to tell others of our faith in Jesus. At least tell them why we live the lifestyle that we do. Our belief makes us different, 'a light unto the world to see.'

When I was a teenager, I started to think about what occupation I would like to work in. I watched the USAF National Guard practice dog fighting in their delta wing fighter jets flying at tree top height over our Pennsylvania ridges! They flew so low that I could read the numbers on the underside of their wings! That's low! They were fast, loud, and exciting to watch! I wondered if I could ever fly a fighter jet, and I would say to myself, "Why not!"

Then I met two local doctors. One reattached my almost severed left ring finger in his office. The other got me through many childhood illnesses. Both asked me, "Would you like to be a doctor some day? Keep your grades up and think about it. You could do this!"

I became the first graduate form my high school to attend the USAF Academy in Colorado. But halfway through the four-year program, I left the academy. I had finally encountered the Living Christ while at the Academy and was uncertain of my future. I was led to become a medic in the Air Force and started by serving in Viet Nam. I watched doctors, nurses, and hospital staff in their daily jobs. I ended up spending twenty years in the US Air Force. They put me through school to become a Physician Assistant instead of a fighter pilot. I had a good career and touched many lives. But finding faith in the Living Jesus at age eighteen was the changing event of my life! It is the subject of this book, and I wish to tell it in much more detail!

REAL CHRISTIANS

I rubbed shoulders with people who had no doubt at all about Jesus still being alive. I asked many of them "How are you so sure?" I got many different answers. Trouble was none of them were true for me! I even took a college course called 'Religions of the World.' I learned an awful lot but was shocked to find that the course did not include Christianity! Why not? Well, the instructor said that we live in a primarily Christian country, so everyone knows Christian beliefs. (My mind shouted "No, we don't!") We ended up studying the words/teachings of each religion's founding father. As I did so, I realized that I only knew Jesus's words that had been taught in each church I had attended. I wanted to know them all so I could better know Jesus. I decided to do my own private study of the words of Jesus, every word that he ever spoke that got recorded.

First, I needed a bible. I did not even own one. There were lots of bibles in the chapel at USAF Academy (blue in color on the outside, 'Revised Standard Version' on the inside) I 'borrowed' one to read and made sure I asked permission so no one would think I had stolen it. If a cadet steals anything, he is kicked out of the Academy! They have a very strict honor code.

Since Jesus's spoken words are only recorded in the New Testament, I started to read the Gospels in order presented: Mathew, Mark, Luke, and last of all John. I quickly realized that I was reading four gospels and getting four views of Christ. The first three were similar, but I did not have a study bible to explain why, just the actual text with very few footnotes. I really focused on what Jesus said, understanding and comparing one Gospel to another.

Much went through my head. I had heard many of Jesus's teachings while attending church but not all of them. Some were pretty tough. Some I grit my teeth and said to myself, "Are you serious Lord? Surely, you are joking!! Love your enemies!" Wow! Jesus also did a lot of miracles. He raised more than one person from the dead! I did not even know that!

THE DAY THAT CHANGED MY LIFE

I had been a regular church goer for greater than five years. I had never been baptized, never joined a church. I had heard quite a few people give their testimonies of believing and how happy they were, and how their lives had changed. I wished for that kind of happiness, just the comfort of knowing Jesus personally. I saw several people I knew go through tremendous change. It seemed effortless for them.

I voiced this to my roommate at the USAF Academy, Gordie, himself a Christian and the son of a minister. I asked him some very hard questions. He said that he did not know all the answers, but he knew a young man who had been a youth minister and he may be able to help me with my questions. He would ask him to come visit me.

Several nights later, there was a knock at my door. When I opened it, he said he was Gordie's friend. I invited him in and asked him his name. He answered me and I thought I heard him say, "My Faith". I said "What? Say your name again please." He said Mike Fay (I may be spelling the last name wrong, but my hearing error gave me goose bumps!). He was very good at explaining things in the gospels for me and we met several times over the next few weeks.

Meanwhile I was working my way through the gospels one at a time, and the Lord's words were burning themselves into me. I could close my eyes and see them.

They touched my soul and I knew it. I read about Thomas and I really felt for him. I felt like I was him. Why, Lord, can I not just make myself believe?

Remember, I had heard the words of Buddha, Confucius, Mohammed, etc. Jesus was a step up. His words were alive! Many times, my prayers ended with: "Help me Jesus! Help me believe you are alive and not just believe in words spoken in the past."

Then I started the Gospel of John one afternoon about five PM. I had no idea what was about to happen. The sun was shining as I opened the bible. The intro to John talks about the word of God and how the Word became flesh and dwelled among us! This gospel was different from the first three and really reached into me beyond what I had ever experienced or felt. To this day, I cannot remember what chapter or verse I was reading but it was in the first few chapters of John. I started to feel a little tired then realized that what I just read did not make sense. A sentence was out of place and not related to the context of the verses I was reading. The sentence was: "Do you know who I am?'

I stopped, stretched, took a drink, and noted that the sun was still up. I reread the section and again at the same place: "Do you know who I am?" But as much as I blinked and stared, those words were not on the paper!! I tried one final time and read the invisible words a third time! I was beyond having goose bumps by then.

I stopped staring at the page, looked straight ahead and said, "Yes!" After all, who else could it be? Whose words had I been reading and studying? Whose life, and death, and resurrection? Whose bible? Who have I been praying to?

I felt tears building in my eyes, but in my mind, I answered him, "Yes Lord Jesus, I know who you are! The Word made flesh! The son of God! You are the Lord! My Lord!"

I blanked my mind and waited. I did not know if anything would follow. I did not wait long! "Do you love me?' The words were in my head but not via my ears.

"Yes, of course!" I thought as tears rolled down my cheeks.

"Then feed my sheep."

I waited for more, but nothing ever came so I looked down and reread the section. No extra words. So, I kept reading, slowly at first then faster and faster. I understood every word. So simple, so strong, nothing to be confused about. Faster and faster until I was flipping pages but reading every word. I skipped nothing!

Not bad for a slow reader! I have never been able to read fast. Never! It had been a hardship in high school and college and still is until today.

I was startled when my roommate touched my shoulder – I jumped in my chair! First thing I noted was that it was pitch black outside. He was saying "It's after ten PM, lights out soon!" I looked down to see I was about to start reading the book of Revelation! I had read the entire new testament from the Book of John to the beginning of Revelation in one sitting! And I understood every word. I had experienced two miracles in one evening! To me both were miraculous! Reading words that were not on the paper and then reading at ten times my normal rate! Neither has ever happened since that night! All so I could have a brief encounter with Jesus. I was not aware how rare such encounters are or what other people experience. I guess I had three miracles in one evening! I now knew that Jesus was definitely still alive!

And from the moment I said "Yes", I felt a warm glow inside me. It was like the word took root and took over. I could not stop smiling and sometimes I would even laugh to myself. Prior to that night, I was known to vent frustration by swearing. Well, the frustration disappeared, and the cussing automatically stopped also! People asked me, "What has changed? Are you in love?"

Yes, I probably was but not with some girl! I was happy for one great reason, I realized that Jesus is physically gone from our world but that he is very much alive! I could relax. Christian belief was real and so was He! The 'Living Lord" had been there the entire time!

I had a new theme to my prayers now! "OK Lord, how am I to feed your sheep?" What does he want me to do? I never got specific instructions. Over time, I have tried to live the faith, tried to set the example, share my love for the Father and His creation. I have also learned to believe in what I cannot see!

DOUBTS

The next couple of years were filled with events and learning experiences. I continued to spend time attending different churches. I did The Navigators program of bible study, and even attended a Bible Church for a time. My friend, Helen Songer, advised me to pick and join a church as a place of service to my fellow Christians. I never forgot her advice.

My older sister decided I was in love with a teacher who had died 2000 years ago! Well, I was! Then doubts started to nag at me. What if my personal miracles were just a type of mental breakdown due to self-imposed stress? Did I fall asleep and dream them? Did I just imagine the unwritten words I had read three times? Was it all mental? What about the speed reading? Could my new faith all be self-induced?

Can we live "Christian" lives without a living Christ? Other religions continue long after their founder's deaths. Why not live the teachings of Christ without the confines of the established religions of Earth? Just live a good life. Without a Lord to direct our lives. Why not?

Soon I decided to live a good life for goodness sake, without any organized religion to guide me. Sounds brave, bold, or just foolish! It was all the above!

For a time, I stopped praying, stopped reading the bible. Then the world started to feel unbalanced. People I loved were letting me down. Others flat out lied to me! Some started stealing from me! Many said untrue things about me.

19

Evil was still active in this world. The unbalancing force was the devil. Pain was all around me! I soon realized I could not manage my personal life without a source of strength! No matter how hard I tried, someone got hurt emotionally. Too soon I realized that every poor decision I made affected two people. The person I hurt and myself. I needed a source of strength stronger than myself!

First thing I prayed about was my doubt. I asked Jesus to forgive my doubt and take it away. Forgive me for not holding tight to my faith and help me build my faith again. A terrible weight left my heart and shoulders that day. I had no doubt that I had been forgiven. I felt Jesus's words: "Keep your eyes on me! Live as I have taught you and you need not 'sink' into doubt again." He knew that it is human to doubt, human to fear. He wants us to seek goodness, and that search will lead us to him.

Prayer returned easily and reading God's Word a joy again. Just holding a bible can make me feel closer to the Lord. As strong as doubt was, faith is stronger! Believing is what we were created for and it feels totally natural!

I felt redeemed and revived. I did not wish to look back, only forward. It would be wrong to say I never had any doubts. I did. I want to share with you that redemption and revival are both as real as Jesus is! He picks us up if we fall because he loves us so. Agape love (selfless spiritual love). The Good Shepherd both calls and sometimes carries His sheep. He calls us all to eternal life with Him. We should follow without hesitation!

FEED MY SHEEP

I was shocked on the day of my conversion when I read later in the book of John that Jesus had said the same words to Peter. "Do you love me?" and "Feed my sheep." I prayed: "How exactly do you want me to do that? When? All the sheep or some of them? Will you guide me Lord or am I on my own with this?"

Well, I never got specific guidance. I have never read words not typed on the page again. I have not heard words in my head again as if spoken there. But sometimes I have received an impression of what Jesus wants me to do in certain circumstances. I have heard what sounds like words in the breeze through tall grasses and the limbs of pine trees. Repeated words sometimes. I followed them and never regretted doing so.

I got married in1976. I officially joined the Catholic Church three years later in1979. Which means I finally was baptized and confirmed. I have done different 'Lay People' jobs in the Catholic Church. I even took a two-year college course that gives me an associate degree in Theology. But the question in me remains: Have I done what the Lord asked me to do?

We are all called to be Christ to others. We are all anointed to serve God at our Baptisms. Does the Lord ask different things of us? I do not know. I do know I could never fill Peter's or any Saint's shoes. As a Catholic, I became an admirer of Mother Theresa of Calcutta. I was also drawn to Saint Francis of Assisi. I became a supporter of the Jesuits and their missions around the world.

Since I am married and the father of five children, becoming a priest at this time would not be possible. So, I focus on serving where I can as a member of my church and as a 4th Degree Knight of Columbus. My occupation for 33 ½ years was as a Physician Assistant. I touched many lives and they were aware of my faith the entire time. Many chose me as their medical care provider because they had heard of my Christian faith.

But have I ever truly given Jesus all I could give? He will be the judge of that someday. Hopefully, he will be merciful and gracious with me. Time will tell. Until then, I will continue to serve as doors open to me. To bring God's love to others is the greatest call.

I wanted to share how I came to believe as I know how special it was. Truly a rare encounter with the risen Lord. And remember, I have never actually seen him that I know of. Mother Theresa used to see Jesus's eyes in the eyes of the dying and the very sick that she took in. How many of us encounter Christ in others and are not aware or it!

One thing for certain, I am glad I answered, "Yes Lord, I know Who you are!"

www.ingramcontent.com/pod-product-compliance
Lightning Source LLC
Chambersburg PA
CBHW041131120626
46547CB00019B/2943